# NO PROBLEM

by

**MEG BROGAN, KATIE DAWSON,
PAUL FITZGERALD, SUSAN FITZGERALD,
JULIET HOWARD, DARLENE HUNT,
SEANA KOFOED, STEVE TRUSSELL**

**Dramatic Publishing**
Woodstock, Illinois • London, England • Melbourne, Australia

## ACKNOWLEDGEMENTS

The authors would like to thank the following people and organizations for their belief in *NO PROBLEM*:

Northwestern School of Speech, Rives Collins, Pam Cooper, Stevenson High School, Rick and Todd, The Kentucky Governors Scholars Program, Peggy Kubert, Russell Kofoed, Patrick McNulty, Bren Dubay, Suzan Zeder, Richelle Pitalo, Abby Epstein, Nina Uziel, Rob Benedict, Steve Shenbaum.

And to
Scot
and Elizabeth
for coming to the party and making it fun.

## WHAT IS NO PROBLEM?

NO PROBLEM is a new play that explores the pressures and concerns of high school life as experienced by five students. The lights go up and we watch them struggle with an essay they must write entitled "I Am Addicted To..."

Suddenly, the play begins to move fluidly through space and time. It travels from the classroom to Jennifer's bedroom, where she stares at her body in front of a mirror, imagining how she would look if she were thinner; to the fraternity where Paula deludes herself into thinking a college student really cares for her; to Jimmy putting his alcoholic mother to bed; and back to the classroom.

The play was developed collaboratively as part of a seminar at Northwestern University, and later as an independent effort. A company of eight worked through research and improvisation to create a fast-paced 45 minutes of innovative theatrical entertainment. The action flows smoothly between past and present, highlighting relationships both in the home and in the classroom, boldly confronting the self destructive behavior which plagues adolescents today, and it does so on their terms. It doesn't just educate teens about specific disorders, it shows them what destructive behavior looks like in themselves and in others. While *NO PROBLEM*'s approach to the issues dealt with is a direct one, the play is entertaining and humorous. That is one of the chief reasons *NO PROBLEM* has been so well received by students as well as adults in the prevention field. Most of all, *NO PROBLEM* is a powerful catalyst for discussion and discovery, as it challenges its audience to question themselves and the choices that they make. By not offering simple solutions, the play promotes independent thought and breaks down barriers of communication between teens and adults. That is why *NO PROBLEM* affects positive change in teens, parents, and teachers alike.

# NO PROBLEM

### A One-Act Play
### For Three Women, Two Men, with doubling

## CHARACTER

JENNIFER

JIMMY

PAULA } high school students

BRIAN

MELISSA

TIME: The present.

SETTING: A high school English class.

The premiere production of *NO PROBLEM* was presented on April 4, 1992 at the Illinois Theatre Association Conference in Wilmette, Illinois. It was directed by Susan Fitzgerald. The cast, in order of appearance, was as follows:

Jennifer ........................... *Darlene Hunt*

Jimmy ............................. *Steve Trussell*

Paula .............................. *Seana Kofoed*

Brian .............................. *Paul Fitzgerald*

Melissa ........................... *Meg Brogan*

# NO PROBLEM

AT RISE: *As the play begins, an alarm clock is heard off-stage. The actors are discovered on stage, frozen in positions appropriate for their characters. As they speak, each actor crosses DC and addresses the audience as he/she narrates for another character. The actors should remain neutral and should not "become" their characters until the school bell is heard. They are aware not only of the audience, but of the presence of the other actors. As they finish speaking, each actor crosses and stands behind the chair of the character about whom they speak.*

JENNIFER. 6:00 a.m. Brian Fenway wakes up. He'll run before breakfast. He has to be in top form for the game tonight.

JIMMY. 6:15. Melissa Anne Bainbridge wakes up. She'll take ten minutes to shower, twenty-five minutes for make-up, and twenty-five minutes for hair. She'll wear her new black dress. It makes her look great. She has a reputation to uphold.

PAULA. 6:30. Jimmy Joseph can't wake up. He'll be late for school. Again.

BRIAN. 6:35. Jennifer Scott wakes up. She'll do 100 sit-ups and have a piece of wheat toast and juice for breakfast. She'll walk to school.

MELISSA. 6:45. Paula Dearborn wakes up. She can't wait to tell Anna about Justin. She's finally in love.

ALL. 7:30. *(The sound of the school bell is heard. It lasts five seconds. ALL students, except JIMMY, freeze.)*

JIMMY. Oh, crap! I'm late for school again!

*(JIMMY grabs his book bag and jacket off of the floor by one of the bookcases. As he begins to move, the other students unfreeze. They begin to interact with normal classroom banter. They should take no notice of JIMMY, who runs upstage and freezes. The students settle into their seats as they interact. Through the chatter, we hear:)*

JENNIFER. Paula, I thought I saw you last night...

*(As JENNIFER says "night", the students in unison look directly out front as an "imaginary" teacher gives the students their assignment. There are some nods of acknowledgement. They hold this pose [though not frozen] for five seconds. They then begin to settle down to the task of writing their essays. JIMMY enters the scene in a frenzy, screaming.)*

JIMMY *(composes himself)*. Terribly sorry. Please put down your pencils and direct your focus this way. I believe we have a bit of a problem. I've just been accosted by a huge space alien of enormous proportions and I believe it's coming this way. It had soft pudding-like hands which I don't think you'd want on any part of your body. It chased me through the air in a ship shaped like a giant rubber.

BRIAN. How would you know what a condom looks like, Jimmy?

JIMMY. Please get your mind out of the gutter. I was referring to a galosh.

MELISSA. Jimmy, you're safe. Ms. Thompson went to the office.

JIMMY. Oh, so what did I miss?

JENNIFER. In-class writing assignment. Essay. Thesis statement: I an addicted to…Use three supports. Due at the end of the period.

MELISSA. You really wrote all that down?

JIMMY. End of the period? I can't do it! The pressure's too great! My hand is cramping up!

JENNIFER. Sit down, Jimmy! You're gonna get us all in trouble.

JIMMY. So sorry…

JENNIFER. Jennifer Scott. Addiction Essay Outline.

Roman numeral I: Topic sentence—People can be addicted to many things:

  A. Good things: work, fitness, etc.

  B. Bad things: drugs, alcohol

Roman numeral II: reasons teenagers are addicts:

  A. They do poorly in school.

  B. They are not happy at home.

Roman numeral III: Me.

  A. I am not an addict.

  B. I do like to chew a lot of gum.

MELISSA. Melissa Anne Bainbridge. *(She freezes.)*

BRIAN. I am addicted to…*(He freezes.)*

*(JIMMY hums the theme to a television game show.)*

PAULA. Dear Anna…*(She freezes.)*

JENNIFER. I chew over fifty pieces of gum a day…

JIMMY. I am addicted to jokes…I'm a very funny guy…*(He freezes.)*

JENNIFER. I started chewing gum a lot when I got my braces off. It's also been a big help when I want to lose a few pounds. I have to stay in shape because I just got a spot on the varsity swim team. I have to work extra hard because I didn't swim all summer. Just ate a lot of dorm food, which isn't the healthiest food in the world. Not even close.

*(By this time, JENNIFER has moved DC with her note-book. JIMMY has gotten a remote control and a bag of chips from the R bookcase. He enters the scene as MI-CHAEL. He mimes turning on the TV.)*

JIMMY/MICHAEL. Hey, where's mom?

JENNIFER. I don't know...Work?

JIMMY/MICHAEL. What's for dinner? *(He offers her the chips. She pushes them away.)*

JENNIFER. I don't know. Could you please turn that off? I'm trying to think.

JIMMY/MICHAEL. What's the matter with you?

JENNIFER. I'm trying to do this stupid application.

JIMMY/MICHAEL. I thought you told mom and dad you were going to lifeguard this summer.

JENNIFER. I discussed it with mom and dad and we decided it would be more beneficial for me to go to the Summer Honors Institute.

JIMMY/MICHAEL. You mean they decided for you.

JENNIFER. No, they didn't. You don't understand. This will look really good on my college applications.

JIMMY/MICHAEL. College applications? Jennifer, you're a sophomore in high school. Don't let mom and dad push you so hard. Besides, you're already Ms. Perfect.

JENNIFER. Right.

JIMMY/MICHAEL. You have perfect grades, perfect atten-
dance, perfect teeth, and I have no doubt that you will also
have the perfect college application. If you want to lifeguard this summer, lifeguard this summer.

JENNIFER. Michael, I'll lifeguard next summer.

JIMMY/MICHAEL. No, you won't. And you're not gonna
lifeguard next summer because next summer mom and dad
will want you to do something else. And you're not gonna
go to the football game Friday night, because Friday night
you have to go to dance class, which you don't really want
to do either! You never do anything you want to do.

JENNIFER. Stop it, Michael. You don't know what you're
talking about.

JIMMY/MICHAEL. You didn't audition for the school play
because dad wanted you to go out for the swim team. You
didn't go out with Josh because mom and dad didn't like
his earring, and you didn't go out for the cheerleading
squad because mom and dad thought it would give colleges
the wrong impression...

JENNIFER *(cutting him off)*. Shut up! *(Pause.)*

JIMMY/MICHAEL. I wouldn't want to spend my summer
eating dorm food and doing math problems. I'm starved.
When mom gets home tell her I went out for pizza. *(He
exits the scene, returns props and takes his seat. He freezes.)*

JENNIFER *(to audience)*. There are over 35 different types of
chewing gum to choose from. I like making my own
choices. *(She sits.)*

*(As JENNIFER sits, PAULA rips a piece of paper from her
notebook. The other students unfreeze.)*

BRIAN. Hey, Paula, what are you writing about?
PAULA. I can't tell you.

BRIAN. What do you mean, you can't tell me? *(PAULA shrugs.)* Fine.

PAULA. I'm not writing my essay.

BRIAN *(as he grabs her paper)*. Well you must be writing something. Let's see.

PAULA. Hey, come on...give it back.

BRIAN. What's the big deal?

PAULA. Nothing...just can I have it back?

MELISSA. Brian, give it back to her.

BRIAN. What, is it a secret?

PAULA. No, it's not a secret. Can I just have it back?

*(As the above conversation transpires, JIMMY crosses between BRIAN and PAULA.)*

JIMMY. Hey, come on, you guys...*(He grabs the paper from BRIAN's hand.)* Interception!

PAULA. Jimmy!

JIMMY. Paula Dearborn's deepest, darkest secrets...I'll start the bidding at ten dollars...*(The students shout out bids as JIMMY waves PAULA's letter around.)*

PAULA *(shouting)*. Jimmy, give it back! *(There is an awkward moment. Then JIMMY gives the letter back. There are giggles from the rest of the class. To JIMMY.)* You know you're not as funny as you think you are.

MELISSA. Ooh, touchy, touchy. *(ALL students, except PAULA, freeze.)*

PAULA *(writing letter)*. Dear Anna. Hi, what's up? Well, I have definitely put Steven behind me and completely forgotten about him. But, I have finally found the right guy! I know last time I told you Steven was the one, but now Justin is. He's my new boyfriend, and he is so great.

We've only known each other a couple of weeks, but I think it's pretty serious. I can't wait for you to meet him.

*(By this point, MELISSA has gotten a package from the prop table. She enters the scene as MOM.)*

MELISSA/MOM. Paula, honey, you have mail. I think it's a package from your father.

PAULA. Excellent! I bet it's the plane tickets.

MELISSA/MOM. It's a little big for plane tickets. But maybe it's something even better.

*(Pause as PAULA waits for her to leave. MELISSA/MOM crosses upstage and freezes, her back to the audience. PAULA opens the package and takes out a letter. BRIAN stands, as DAD.)*

BRIAN/DAD. Dear Paula. Hi, pumpkin. How's it going? We've got great news. Cindy's going to have a baby. She's expecting in April, and the doctor thinks she should avoid stress over the holidays. We've decided to take it easy this December so I think we'll have to postpone your visit again. Maybe over the summer would be better, or next fall when you can see your new baby brother or sister. We hope you like the present. Love, Dad...P.S. Cindy sends her love.

*(As BRIAN/DAD sits and freezes, MELISSA/MOM un-freezes and crosses to PAULA.)*

MELISSA/MOM. So, what did your father have to say?

PAULA. Well, actually, I don't think I'm gonna go this time. Because he's really busy at work and all. So we think it would be better for me to come over the summer because I won't have school and I can stay longer and the weather's better and...

MELISSA/MOM. Sure. Of course...Honey, you know, if you're not going to visit your dad over vacation you could still enter your sketches in that art show you were talking about.

PAULA. No, they're not that good.

MELISSA/MOM. Paula, they are good.

PAULA. Okay, I'll think about it. *(Pause.)*

MELISSA/MOM. So, what's in the box?

PAULA. Oh, I didn't look. *(She opens the package and pulls out a too-small shirt.)*

MELISSA/MOM. Oh...it looks a little small. Well, maybe we can exchange it, or maybe it would fit your sister...You know, Paula, your dad never was very good at sizing things...Look, why don't I take it to the store with me and see if...

PAULA. No, that's okay. I want to keep it.

MELISSA/MOM. Sure. Whatever you want. *(She crosses back to her seat and freezes.)*

PAULA. I have a whole closet full of clothes that don't fit me. *(She sits and continues writing her letter.)* Anyway, it looks like I won't be going to San Francisco over break... my dad's really bummed, but Justin says he can't bear to be without me for two weeks. *(She freezes.)*

MELISSA *(unfreezes)*. Although I wouldn't consider myself addicted to anything, I am in the habit of going shopping a few times a week. Actually, I go every chance I get. *(She freezes.)*

JENNIFER *(unfreezes)*. For me, chewing gum has gone from a habit to an art. *(She freezes.)*

JIMMY *(as he wanders around the classroom).* I am so very, ultimately, outrageously, out-of-this-world, dynamitely happy that I get to write this paper. I love this paper. You see, *(He sings.)* you might as well face, it I'm addicted to love! Actually, I am addicted to large, robust women, of Armenian descent, who like to eat fish raw and…Oh, shit. *(Crosses out what he's written.)* I am addicted to…jokes. I'm a very funny guy.

*(The following scene is played twice. Each time, the students' movements should be exactly the same, except for JIMMY. The movements should be strange, unnatural, and exaggerated. In the original production, the gestures were bold, staccato, and almost robotic. The actors should make reference to JIMMY's empty seat, as though he is actually sitting there, taking part in the conversation. They never actually notice JIMMY, who is standing behind them. During the first scene, JIMMY responds in a naturalistic manner. The second time, JIMMY joins the strange surrealism of the scene. Never should we think that we are actually in the classroom. Unfreeze.)*

BRIAN. Oh my God, isn't Friday night Parents' Night?

MELISSA. Why else would I be doing my work?

JIMMY. I hope my mom hasn't heard about it.

JENNIFER. Are everybody's parents coming?

PAULA. I doubt it. Are yours?

JENNIFER. My parents organized it. Just kidding!

MELISSA. My parents will be there. It's their annual parental appearance.

PAULA. Yeah, my mom will be there.

MELISSA. What about you, Jimmy, is your dad as funny as you are?

JIMMY. My dad is dead. *(Laughter.)* I really miss him. *(More laughter.)*

BRIAN. What about your mom? Will she be there?

JIMMY. I hope she doesn't go. I'd be really embarrassed. *(More laughter.)*

BRIAN. Why, can't she get a date?

JIMMY. I'd rather not talk about it. It's kind of personal. *(More laughter. Freeze. JIMMY crosses back to his desk.)* No one wants to hear your problems.

*(Unfreeze.)*

BRIAN. Oh my God. Isn't Friday night Parents' Night?

MELISSA. Why else would I be doing my work?

JIMMY. Parents' Night. The next best thing to Disney World!

JENNIFER. Are everybody's parents coming?

PAULA. I doubt it. Are yours?

JENNIFER. My parents organized it. Just kidding!

PAULA. Yeah. My mom will be there.

MELISSA. What about you, Jimmy. Is your dad as funny as you are?

JIMMY. Haven't you heard of my dad? David Letterman? *(Laughter.)* Actually, I'm not sure if that's true. My mom might have made it up! *(More laughter.)*

BRIAN. What about your mom. Will she be there?

JIMMY. Friday night? Friday night she has to make an appearance on "Studs." *(More laughter.)*

BRIAN. Why, can't she get a date?

JIMMY. Well, she's a little short on cash right now. *(More laughter. ALL freeze except JIMMY.)* No one wants to hear your problems. It's easier just to make them laugh.

*(Unfreeze. BRIAN picks a piece of paper off of the floor. He throws it to JIMMY.)*

BRIAN. Jimmy, go out!

JIMMY. He goes out for the long pass, he connects! *(JIMMY backs up into MELISSA.)* Heal me with a kiss.

MELISSA. Please! You're drooling on my dress!

BRIAN. I wouldn't worry about it. She has a million of them.

JENNIFER. I love that dress.

MELISSA. Thanks, I got it last week.

*(JENNIFER pops her gum loudly. PAULA rips a piece of paper out of her notebook.)*

BRIAN. God, I hate it when she does that.

PAULA. I'm sorry.

BRIAN. No, I mean Jennifer and her gum disorder.

MELISSA. Brian!

JIMMY. I feel like there's not enough love in this classroom.
*(ALL freeze except BRIAN.)*

BRIAN *(reading from essay)*. I am addicted to winning. I come from a family of winners. My father has set high standards for my brothers and me to live by. *(He freezes)*.

MELISSA *(unfreezes)*. Shopping is a great way to relax and a great activity to do with friends. On a typical Saturday, I go to the mall, have lunch, walk around, get a make-over, talk to friends, and try on the $5000 dresses in the ritzy dress store on the top floor. My mother always used to say to me:

JENNIFER/MOM. Melissa, remember, if you look good, you'll feel good!

MELISSA. So, I started small...earrings. I have over 200 pair. I try to pick up a new pair whenever I'm out.

*(MELISSA, by this point, is out of her chair. JENNIFER [as MELISSA's mom] has moved into MELISSA's chair and begins applying make-up. MELISSA gets her bag from the bookcase R, and begins to exit.)*

JENNIFER/MOM. Melissa, where are you going?

MELISSA. Out!

JENNIFER/MOM. You're not going anywhere. You're staying home with Max this afternoon. We discussed it last night.

MELISSA. Mom...I told Meredith I'd meet her at the mall. I'll be home before dinner.

JENNIFER/MOM. You'll have to call her and tell her you can't make it.

MELISSA. Why do I have to watch him?

JENNIFER/MOM. Because I have an important meeting with a client and then your father and I have to be at that benefit downtown. *(She turns to MELISSA.)* I thought I told you to throw those jeans away.

MELISSA. Mom, these are my favorite pair.

JENNIFER/MOM. You look like a homeless person. What will people think?

MELISSA. I don't care what people think!

JENNIFER/MOM. I do. Your father and I work too hard to have you traipsing around in ripped clothing.

MELISSA. Fine, mom, I'll take them off!

JENNIFER/MOM. Melissa, what has gotten into you lately? I don't know where you've picked up this attitude, but I will not tolerate it in my house. Do you understand?

MELISSA. Fine.

JENNIFER/MOM. Melissa, is there a problem?

MELISSA. Well, I just don't see why I have to watch him all the time...I'm not his mother.

JENNIFER/MOM. Because this is a family. *(Pause.)*

MELISSA. What am I supposed to do for dinner?

JENNIFER/MOM. You can order a pizza. I'll leave some money on the counter.

MELISSA. At the mall, you can always get people to help you...to pay attention to you...They have to. It's their job

*(Unfreeze.)*

JENNIFER. Melissa, are you going to the game tonight?

MELISSA. Of course. And we're going to win. Right, Brian?

BRIAN. Do I ever lose?

JIMMY. Actually, Brian, I heard you fumbled with Yvonne at Jack's party last weekend...threw a couple of missed passes at Mary Beth...Didn't score that night! *(Laughter. PAULA laughs very loudly. Everyone looks at her.)*

PAULA. It's only football...

MELISSA. She's so clueless! *(ALL freeze, except PAULA.)*

PAULA *(back to letter)*. This girl I've been hanging out with thinks she can get me a spot on the prom committee. I'd have to drop my art classes, but she says there's a lot of cool people doing it. *(Freezes.)*

BRIAN *(unfreezes)*. Some people don't understand the importance of competition. If you didn't already know, Mrs. Thompson, my father was an All-American QB for the Buckeyes back in '64, and my older brother Rodney plays basketball for Michigan. My dad always says:

JIMMY/DAD *(stands)*. Once you get labeled a loser, it follows you the rest of your life.

*(As BRIAN continues, JIMMY gets "dad's" baseball cap from the bookcase R and crosses back to his seat.*

*JIMMY/DAD's lines are said straight out as though he were watching BRIAN play football.)*

BRIAN. When I was ten years old my father coached my Little League football team. I played receiver...

JIMMY/DAD. Keep your eye on the ball, Brian!

BRIAN. We went over plays in the backyard...

JIMMY/DAD. Pay attention, Brian!

BRIAN. Everyday.

JIMMY/DAD. Again, Brian!

BRIAN. Our first game came—*(As BRIAN speaks this line, PAULA, JENNIFER and MELISSA look directly out and quietly chant his name. They are his fans, cheering him on.)*—and the first and only pass that got thrown to me...

JIMMY/DAD. Watch the ball, Brian! *(The GIRLS stop chanting.)*

BRIAN. I dropped.

JIMMY/DAD. Dammit, Brian!

*(JIMMY/DAD throws his hat on the desk, and crosses upstage behind BRIAN's chair, his back to the audience. He freezes. BRIAN crosses downstage to JIMMY's chair. He sits, holding his dad's baseball cap.)*

BRIAN. On the way home from the game, my father didn't say a word. He wasn't so much mad as he was disappointed.

JIMMY/DAD *(knocks on the back of BRIAN's chair).* Brian, can I come in? *(He crosses to BRIAN.)* First of all, Brian, let's not have any crying. Crying is for little girls. Now when you fail and fall short of your goals, you don't cry about it. You do what you have to do to make sure it doesn't happen again. So you missed the pass. So next time you run faster, watch the ball closer. We'll spend extra time after practice going over plays.

BRIAN. Yes sir.

JIMMY/DAD. All of your brothers have been winners and made this family proud. I'd hope you'd expect the same of yourself.

BRIAN. I'll try, sir.

JIMMY/DAD. Well you'll have to do more than try! I want you to succeed, Brian. You can't settle for second if you want to come out on top.

BRIAN. Yes sir.

JIMMY/DAD. I only want what's best for you, Brian. Once you get labeled a loser—

BRIAN. —it follows you the rest of your life.

JIMMY/DAD (*pats BRIAN on the back*). I'll see you down at dinner. (*JIMMY/DAD crosses upstage and freezes. BRIAN watches him exit, stands and crosses back to his seat. He sits.*)

BRIAN. I have tried my entire life to be the best at whatever I do. I am a winner.

(*JENNIFER pops her gum. Unfreeze. JIMMY crosses to JENNIFER and watches as she plays with her gum wrappers. He begins to play with the wrappers, obviously trying to annoy her. The rest of the class watches.*)

JENNIFER. What!

BRIAN. Jennifer, why do you do that?

JENNIFER. Do what?

BRIAN. You chew 800 pieces of gum a day, and we all have to sit here and listen to you pop it. And look what you're doing to the wrappers.

MELISSA. Brian, leave her alone.

BRIAN. I'm sorry, but that's not normal. *(JIMMY spits out a gum wrapper.)*

JENNIFER. I don't think it's any of your business what I do with my gum.

BRIAN. Well you make it my business when you pop it in my face all day!

JENNIFER. I'm not even near you!

BRIAN. Whatever...

JENNIFER *(to MELISSA)*. He's such a jerk. I can't believe you're friends with him.

MELISSA. At least I don't sit home on Friday nights.

JENNIFER. For your information, I have dance classes on Friday nights. Not that you would know that, not that you would know anything about me! So don't pretend that you do! Just leave me alone!

*(During this, JENNIFER has stood. As she tries to sit, JIMMY takes her seat. The following is an imitation of an Alcoholics Anonymous meeting, with JIMMY as both counselor and member.)*

JIMMY. Hi, my name is Jennifer.

—Hi, Jennifer.

OK, this is a little difficult for me to bring up, you know, in front of the group.

—It's OK, Jennifer. We all have problems here.

Well, I like to chew a lot of gum, and there's this really mean girl in my class and she's friends with this dumb jock. *(PAULA laughs)*. And then there's this other girl who laughs really loud...we're not sure why. And...

—It's OK, Jennifer, you can tell us...

See, I'm in love with this really hot guy named Jimmy and I just can't control myself when he's around!

JENNIFER (*pushes JIMMY out of her chair and sits*). I'm in control! (*ALL freeze, except PAULA.*)

PAULA (*continuing letter*). Anyway, how was your weekend? Mine was awesome. We went to this keg party at a fraternity. No one had any idea we were in high school. I met this really hot guy. You would die if you saw him. I went back to the frat a couple of days later and we hung out. He's really cool…

(*During PAULA's letter, the other characters have gathered in a group and chat as if at a party. PAULA crosses to them.*)

PAULA. Hey, Todd!

(*JIMMY/TODD crosses to her as the others watch. There is an awkward pause.*)

JIMMY/TODD. I'm sorry…I don't remember your name.

PAULA. Paula. Remember…I met you at the party last weekend.

JIMMY/TODD. Oh, yeah! You were the girl who had one drink and was falling all over the place. Glad to see you made it home in one piece.

PAULA. Yeah, it was a wild night. (*Pause.*)

JIMMY/TODD. So, what're you doing here?

PAULA. I was just up visiting a friend and I thought I'd come by and say hi, and see if you still wanted to go out Friday night.

JIMMY/TODD. Friday night?

PAULA. Remember you wanted to see that movie, and we talked about going Friday night?

JIMMY/TODD. Oh, wow! I totally forgot. I've got exams coming up. I really can't go out.

PAULA. Oh. OK. That's cool. Maybe we could go next weekend...after your exams.

JIMMY/TODD. I don't really know what I'm doing yet.

PAULA. Well I can come by next week.

JIMMY/TODD. OK. Whatever...Have fun with your friend.

PAULA. Huh? Oh, yeah...thanks. *(JIMMY/TODD returns to the group. They freeze.)* So it looks like we're gonna go out next weekend.

*(Unfreeze. BRIAN and JIMMY return to their seats. JENNIFER wanders towards the bookcase L in preparation for the next scene.)*

MELISSA. Didn't you hear what I said?

PAULA. What?

MELISSA. I said I like your shirt.

PAULA. Oh, thanks.

MELISSA. You know, Paula, I was looking at you, and I think you'd look a lot better with your hair up. *(Pause.)* Not that it looks bad down, or anything. *(Pause. PAULA sits. ALL freeze. To audience.)* I just have a thing about hair.

*(She sits as JENNIFER/MOM picks up a Hair and Make-up Barbie from the prop table. The following scene should be played straight out, with neither character looking at each other. When MELISSA says "mommy", PAULA, BRIAN, and JIMMY softly hum "Happy Birthday", but never break their freeze.)*

JENNIFER/MOM. Missy, sweetheart, look what mommy has for you!

MELISSA. Oh, mommy! A Hair and Make-up Barbie! I love it! Thank you so much!

JENNIFER/MOM. Careful, sweetheart. We don't want to get mommy all dirty. Now when you're learning to use make-up you can practice on Barbie so you'll know what looks good. Remember, you should never scrimp or use anything but the best brands. Even Barbie knows the value of quality.

MELISSA. Are we going to light the candles on the fancy bakery cake now?

JENNIFER/MOM. Actually, honey, mommy has to go out for a little while, but Amy's coming over to watch you. You like Amy, don't you? *(JENNIFER puts Barbie back and returns to her seat. She freezes and the humming stops.)*

MELISSA. We didn't have time to light the candles on the cake, but mom said we'd do it later.

*(Unfreeze as JIMMY groans.)*

MELISSA. Jimmy, what is your problem?

JIMMY. I can't do this. This assignment is so stupid. I'm just making up a dumb addiction.

JENNIFER. That's OK. If you don't have a real one, just make one up. That's what I'm doing.

BRIAN. Yeah, me too.

MELISSA *(to JENNIFER)*. You know who should really be writing this essay? Brian...Brian...he's on the football team.

BRIAN. I don't know what you're talking about.

JIMMY. Wait, I want to hear this.

MELISSA. It's Allen Heckman!

JENNIFER. What's wrong with Allen Heckman?

MELISSA. Well, we all know that he hasn't been in school lately. It's not because he has mono like everyone says...He's in rehab!

PAULA. For what?

MELISSA *(sarcastically)*. For chocolate...for drugs!

BRIAN. Melissa, I told you not to say anything.

PAULA. Are you sure?

BRIAN. Look, it's nobody's business!

PAULA. Are you sure? I mean, I don't really know him that well, but he never seemed like he did drugs.

JENNIFER. Well, he can't help it if he's an addict. That's what an addiction is, that's what we're writing about.

MELISSA. I read somewhere that rehab costs over two thousand dollars a day. I'm sorry, but that seems a little excessive to me.

*(BRIAN slams his books down in anger. JIMMY stands and does the same, mocking him.)*

BRIAN. Can't you take anything seriously?

JIMMY. Sorry. *(ALL freeze, except JIMMY.)* Some people just can't take a joke. *(He crosses to the bookcase R, picks up a phone and dials.)* Hi, Mr. Hemsley...Hi...this is Jimmy Joseph, Elizabeth Joseph's son. My mom can't come to work today. She's really sick. The doctor says it's a bad flu but hopefully it'll be gone in a couple of days... yeah...Believe me, you wouldn't want to see her. She's got pus running out of her nose and slime dripping out of her eyes. And her skin is like...sorry...I was just kidding... what?...OK...I'll tell her. Yes sir. Bye.

*(BRIAN/ROY has entered the scene and heard JIMMY's phone call. JIMMY returns the phone to the table.)*

BRIAN/ROY. Making excuses for her again, huh? You call up work and make up another one of your stupid stories?

JIMMY. Roy, will you take me to school?

BRIAN/ROY. Why do you waste your time dealing with that?

JIMMY. Roy, I really need you to take me to school.

BRIAN/ROY. Forget it. I'm not taking you. You smell like her puke. *(He begins to leave, JIMMY follows him.)*

JIMMY. You have to take me. I've been late every day this week.

BRIAN/ROY. That's your problem. You waste all your time dealing with that pathetic woman.

JIMMY. Roy...she's your mother...and besides, it's almost her and dad's anniversary time again and she's depressed.

BRIAN/ROY. She's not depressed. She's a drunk. Get out of my face! I have a headache, I'm going back to bed. *(He crosses back to his seat. He freezes.)*

JIMMY. Roy! You have to take me to school! Roy! *(JIMMY returns to his desk. Sits.)* The greatest comics have spent years on their craft working their routines out in front of the toughest crowds.

*(Everyone unfreeze as JIMMY hums a cartoon song. He draws a picture and shows PAULA.)*

JIMMY. Paula, do you know what this is? This is my dog Spot. I take Spot wherever I go. Spot is my best friend. Come on, Spot, let's go for a walk. Woof, woof. Oh no! Look out, Spot! Big truck coming fast! No! No! *(He wads up the paper, throws it on the floor.)* He's dead! There's a dead dog in the middle of the road!

PAULA. I one a dead dog.

MELISSA. I two a dead dog.

JENNIFER. I three a dead dog. *(Pause. The students look to BRIAN, hoping he will join in the game.)*

BRIAN. I four a dead dog.

JIMMY. I five a dead dog.

PAULA. I six a dead dog.

MELISSA. I seven a dead dog.

JENNIFER. I eight a dead dog. *(ALL students look at JENNIFER and laugh.)*

MELISSA. You ate him? I've never seen you eat anything! *(ALL freeze, looking at JENNIFER. She is shaken.)*

JENNIFER *(to audience)*. I always unwrap a piece of gum in three steps, And I never chew a single piece of gum longer than 25 minutes. My usual average is around four packs an hour.

MELISSA *(does not break the freeze as she speaks)*. If you were thinner, you'd be more popular.

JENNIFER. What?

MELISSA *(unfreezes)*. Do you have another pen? *(JENNIFER gives her a pen. MELISSA freezes.)*

JENNIFER. I think certain kinds of gum are definitely meant for certain times of day. Early morning is mint to get you awake and going. Lunches are banana-berry or grape or watermelon, something more filling. After school is cinnamon, when you start dragging around 4:00, and before you go to bed, it's back to mint. It sort of rounds out your day.

BRIAN *(does not break the freeze as he speaks)*. If you were thinner, I'd ask you out.

JENNIFER. Gum chewing is a very practical addiction. Unlike smoking, you can chew gum almost anywhere. At home, at school, even in the library if you're quiet. You can chew gum when you're exercising to make the time pass quickly.

*(By this point, JENNIFER has crossed downstage. She begins to do sit-ups. Note: The following scene is meant to illustrate the voices that JENNIFER hears in her head, telling her she is fat. These "voices" are personified through the other students. In the original production, the students were active participants in the scene.)*

JENNIFER. 45...46...47...48...

JIMMY. If you were thinner, you'd be a lot more fun.

JENNIFER *(stands as though looking in a mirror)*. It's not working. You're not getting any smaller. What were you thinking when you ate that cookie with Melissa today? You are so ugly—

BRIAN. If you were thinner, people would notice you.

JENNIFER. —I can't believe she even talks to you.

MELISSA. If you were thinner, you'd be a lot more popular.

JENNIFER. Jennifer, tomorrow you'll do better. *(She pulls on the skin on her thighs, under her chin, and at her waist.)* You look like a fat old woman.

BRIAN. If you were thinner, I'd ask you out.

JENNIFER. It's just hanging on you, hanging on your arms. Two inches off at least...

PAULA. If you were thinner, you'd be pretty.

BRIAN. If you were thinner, you'd be a better swimmer.

JENNIFER. Dammit, Jennifer, look at yourself! Would you just look at yourself? Look at your thighs, those fat hips.

JIMMY. If you were thinner, people would envy you.

JENNIFER. Jennifer, you are disgusting!

MELISSA & PAULA. You are so disgusting!

JENNIFER. You are so disgusting! How can anyone stand to look at you?

JIMMY. I can't stand to look at you!

JENNIFER. You can't go to parties like this. You can't wear pretty clothes.

BRIAN & JIMMY. You can control it!

JENNIFER. You can control it! You can do it. You have to be thin. Jennifer will lose six pounds by next Wednesday. She will walk to school every day this week and will not eat lunch or breakfast.

ALL *(but JENNIFER).* If you were thinner, you'd be happy. If you were thinner, everything would be all right. *(They return to their seats and freeze.)*

JENNIFER. You can chew gum when you first wake up in the morning and right before you go to bed at night. I chew gum when I'm hungry and it fills me up.

*(She sits. Unfreeze. JIMMY sits in his chair, meditating loudly.)*

JIMMY. UMMMM, I am addicted to UMMM, meditation and, UMMMbilical cords.

JENNIFER. Jimmy, if you don't write your essay, you're going to fail. *(Freeze.)*

PAULA *(reads).* Did I mention in my last letter that we now have open lunch? We can go anywhere off campus as long as we're back by sixth period. Me and my best friend Julie are always looking for an adventure! Julie is class secretary and head cheerleader. She's really cool. Her boyfriend is a junior, and has a car, so we usually go to McDonald's over lunch. Sometimes we even cut sixth period...

*(JENNIFER/JULIE stands and crosses, as if to exit. PAULA stands, crosses to her.)*

PAULA. Hey Julie, wait up! What are you doing for lunch?

JENNIFER/JULIE. I don't know. Why?

PAULA. Do you want to go to McDonald's or something?

JENNIFER/JULIE. Actually, Joey and I are going for pizza.

PAULA. That's cool.

JENNIFER/JULIE. Well, there's a couple of people going. There's really not room in the car.

PAULA. Oh. OK.

JENNIFER/JULIE. Oh...and Paula..My mom kind of mentioned last night that maybe you shouldn't call so late. My parents go to bed by eleven.

*(JENNIFER/JULIE exits scene and freezes by her desk. As PAULA says her next line, BRIAN crosses behind her and enters the scene as SCOTT.)*

PAULA. I thought you liked me.

BRIAN/SCOTT. I do like you, Paula.

PAULA *(turns. She is face to face with SCOTT. He caresses her hair)*. You do?

BRIAN/SCOTT. Yeah. Hey, listen, why don't we get out of here. My folks are out of town, we can go back to my place. You can crash there.

PAULA. Well, I don't know if I should leave my friend...

BRIAN/SCOTT. She'll be all right. *(Pause.)* What's the matter...haven't you ever spent the night with a guy before?

PAULA *(uncomfortable giggle)*. Yeah...all the time...No, I mean...not all the time, but...*(Pause.)* I just don't know if I should leave my friend.

BRIAN/SCOTT. OK, that's cool. *(He crosses towards his seat.)*

PAULA. No, wait. I'll go. *(BRIAN/SCOTT smiles and freezes.)* He says he likes me a lot.

*(PAULA, JENNIFER, and BRIAN sit in unison as the others unfreeze.)*

JIMMY *(sings)*. Ummmm...forgettable, in every way.

JENNIFER. Jimmy, you'll never get into college.

MELISSA. There are more important things than getting into college.

BRIAN *(sarcastically)*. Like shopping!

JIMMY. I'm not going to college. I'm going to be a stand-up comedian with my own talk show.

BRIAN. Right!

PAULA. That sounds really cool.

JIMMY. Well, you can be on my show, Paula.

PAULA. Really?

MELISSA. No, put me on your show!

BRIAN. As what?

MELISSA. As a very famous celebrity.

JIMMY *(sings theme to a late-night talk-show)*. I just flew in from L.A. and, boy, are my arms tired. Badup-bum! But seriously, folks. We've got a great show for you tonight. Esmerelda and her wacky poodles are here...Barney the purple dinosaur is here. And, the woman we all love, for no reason in particular, Melissa Ann Bainbridge!

MELISSA. Thanks, James. *(Looks into "camera.")* Hi, Brian!

JIMMY. So tell us, Ms. Bainbridge, have you always been a celebrity?

MELISSA. Oh yes. In high school I was the most popular girl. I was even voted Homecoming Queen. *(To the others, under her breath.)* Vote for me!

JIMMY. Well, your parents must have been very proud of you.

MELISSA. Proud? Proud of their million-dollar home, their three-car garage, the money they gave to charity...Proud of me? No, I don't think so.

JIMMY. Am I to understand that your home life is, how shall I put this, less than satisfying?

MELISSA. Let's talk about my home life for a moment, shall we, James? Mr. Irwin J. and Mrs. Bev Ann Bainbridge. You know, James, I'd love to talk about them, but I just can't seem to remember them. I mean, between board meetings, dinner parties, time on the golf course...who had time to notice me?

BRIAN. That's not fair, Melissa.

MELISSA. Oh, but I'm not being completely fair, James. We did spend some fabulous quality time quibbling over who would watch my little brother Max.

BRIAN. Melissa, get over it! I've met your parents. They're perfectly nice people.

MELISSA. Actually, I don't think Max has ever even met our parents...But he is a convenient tax write-off!

BRIAN. Melissa, you know your parents care about you.

MELISSA. Not as much as they care about their china pattern.

BRIAN. You are so spoiled. You have no right to complain. They give you everything you want.

MELISSA. Do you really believe that?...Thank you, James, it's been a pleasure but I have an essay to finish. (*ALL but MELISSA freeze.*) I was really disappointed in Meredith last week. Some people are so afraid to take risks. Meredith is just so insecure. She can't take a chance, face a challenge, live a little.

(*PAULA/MEREDITH rises.*)

MELISSA. People like that never get anywhere...*(MELISSA crosses to the bookcase, L, and picks up earrings. PAULA picks up purse from bookcase, R.)* Hey, Mer, check out these earrings.

PAULA/MEREDITH. Oh, Melissa, they're perfect. They're exactly what I need for my dress. Do you think they're real?

MELISSA. Real? Let's see. *(She bites them.)*

PAULA/MEREDITH. Melissa...

MELISSA. What? This is how you figure out if they're real. You bite them.

PAULA/MEREDITH. I don't think you're supposed to do that. You haven't paid for them.

MELISSA. I have now.

PAULA/MEREDITH. You can't buy a pair of $300 earrings.

MELISSA. Who said anything about buying? *(She puts them into PAULA's purse.)*

PAULA/MEREDITH. Hey! Melissa...

MELISSA. Just act normal. Here he comes. *(She looks at the imaginary "sales clerk.")* Oh, yes, you can. Do you have those in silver? OK. We'll wait.

PAULA/MEREDITH. If you want them, you take them! *(Hands earrings back to MELISSA.)*

MELISSA. Fine. Whatever. You said you wanted to dress like me.

PAULA/MEREDITH. I'll meet you outside.

MELISSA. OK. *(She watches PAULA/MEREDITH leave, sit and freeze. She puts the earrings into her pocket and speaks to "clerk.")* No, I decided against that pair, they weren't what I wanted after all. *(To audience.)* I shop, because in the mall, I can do whatever I want and that's very exciting.

*(Unfreeze.)*

BRIAN. Melissa, I don't know why you think your parents are so much worse than anybody else's.

JIMMY. What do you know about anyone else's family?

BRIAN. Oh, you're one to talk, Jimmy. I'm sure your house is just full of pain and sorrow.

JIMMY. No, it's real fun. I get to put my mom to bed every night.

BRIAN. You just can't be serious, can you?

JIMMY. I was being serious!

BRIAN. Yeah, right.

JENNIFER. What's wrong with your mom?

JIMMY. Nothing, just forget it.

*(ALL but JIMMY and PAULA freeze. PAULA/MOM gets a whisky bottle and a glass from the bookcase, R. She staggers to JIMMY's chair and sits.)*

PAULA/MOM. Jimmy...

JIMMY. Mom, what are you doing up?

PAULA/MOM. Oh, Jimmy. I'm so glad you're home. Come over here. We're having a celebration. Today is a very special day, Jimmy!

JIMMY. Come on, mom. It's time to go to bed.

PAULA/MOM. Jimmy, wait! I want to tell you what today is...

JIMMY. Mom, stand up!

PAULA/MOM. Today is your father's and my anniversary. Happy Anniversary! Let's have a toast.

JIMMY. Come on. It's late. It's time to go upstairs.

PAULA/MOM. Jimmy, I love you. You are my only friend left in the whole world. Have I told you how much I love you? Come here, Jimmy, give your mom a hug.

JIMMY. Mom, stop it! Stand up!

PAULA/MOM. No. I want to go out! I want to go dancing! Where are my car keys?

JIMMY. No, mom! It's late. You're going to bed!

PAULA/MOM. Jimmy, don't talk to me like that!

JIMMY. I'm sorry, mom...let's just go upstairs. *(She staggers.)* Are you going to be sick? Come on...I'll get you to the bathroom. *(JIMMY helps PAULA/MOM to her seat. She sits and freezes as PAULA. He picks up the whisky bottle and glass and returns them to the bookcase.)* Sometimes I just want to leave her there.

*(Unfreeze. Note: The following scene is a combination of new lines and moments from previous scenes. The scene should be kept in motion, with the student stopping only during the "flashback lines" to form "snapshots" from previous scenes. The more closely these moments resemble the moments from the original scenes, the better. The end result should be a visual montage of the play.)*

MELISSA. Not everyone is addicted to something.

JIMMY. Yeah.

JENNIFER. I like making my own choices.

JIMMY/MICHAEL *(to JENNIFER)*. If you want to lifeguard this summer, lifeguard this summer!

BRIAN. As long as they're the right choices.

JENNIFER. What does that mean?

BRIAN. You don't want to slack off. You know, become a screw-up.

PAULA. Like Allen Heckman!

BRIAN. You don't even know Allen Heckman!

PAULA. I know him...We're friends.

JIMMY/TODD *(to PAULA)*. I'm sorry, I don't remember your name.

*(PAULA and MELISSA/MOM step forward.)*

MELISSA/MOM. Paula, if you're not sick you have to go to school!

PAULA. I'm not going! I hate it!

*(Unfreeze.)*

JENNIFER. You just have to take control of your own life.

ALL *(but JENNIFER, to JENNIFER)*. If you were thinner!

BRIAN. Or at least your gum! *(JIMMY sings theme to a late-night talk-show.)*

MELISSA. Well we can't all be perfect.

JIMMY. So tell me, have you always been a celebrity?

JENNIFER. I never said I was perfect!

JIMMY. Nobody's perfect!

PAULA/MOM. Jimmy, you're my best friend in the whole world.

JENNIFER. Jimmy, you're such a loser!

MELISSA. Oh, and you're such a winner?

BRIAN. There's nothing wrong with wanting to win.

JIMMY/DAD *(to BRIAN)*. Once you get labeled a loser...

JENNIFER. I didn't think we were talking about winning.

MELISSA. Don't get him started on winning. It's all he ever thinks about. *(ALL but BRIAN freeze.)*

BRIAN. Some people just don't understand the importance of competition. *(He crosses to the bookcase, R, and picks up gym bag.)* Sometimes when I lose a game, it's like the end of the world.

*(BRIAN takes a towel out of the bag and throws it to the ground. He begins to pack his bag. MELISSA crosses up-*

*stage, and enters the scene as CARA. She sneaks up on BRIAN.)*

MELISSA/CARA. Brian! *(BRIAN jumps, startled. He glares at her. Pause.)* There you are...Hey, are you ready to go? *(Pause.)* Jay Irving's having a bunch of people over. I thought we could go over there before the dance...

BRIAN. No. Sorry. I don't feel like it.

MELISSA/CARA. Brian...what are you talking about? Come on, Brian...we had plans. *(Pause.)* Come on, everyone's going to be there and they'll be wondering why we're so late...So come on, let's go. *(She touches his arm. He pushes her hand away.)*

BRIAN. I said no! I'm not going! I don't feel like it!

MELISSA/CARA. What's up with you?

BRIAN. What's up with me? Well, for starters, I just lost a football game.

MELISSA/CARA. Brian, *you* didn't lose...the whole team lost. Besides, Southport was just playing a little better tonight, that's all. It's no big deal.

BRIAN *(yelling)*. No big deal? What the hell are you talking about? Do you hear yourself? We lost, Cara, do you understand? This isn't girls' tennis, or something! We lost a football game! We failed!

MELISSA/CARA. For God's sake, Brian, when are you going to grow out of this? You pull this crap every time things don't go exactly your way...every time you don't have one of your precious wins. You can't always win, you know, Brian. *(She exits.)*

BRIAN *(yelling after her)*. Oh yeah? Well show me a good loser, and I'll show you someone who sits the bench! *(To the audience.)* Once you get labeled a loser, it follows you the rest of your life.

*(Unfreeze.)*

JIMMY *(reading BRIAN's paper and making fun of him).*
Once you get labeled a loser, it follows you for the rest of
your life. Awwww...Hi, everyone. My name is Brian.

JENNIFER *(overlapping).* Is that your essay? I think that's
good.

OTHERS. Hi, Brian!

MELISSA. Welcome to Losers Anonymous!

JIMMY. Don't call him a loser. It'll follow him the rest of his
life!

BRIAN. That's right, Jimmy. Go ahead and make fun of me.
You think I have a problem because I like to win, because
I like being the star of the football team, because I'm going
to make something of myself?

JIMMY. Yeah, basically...

BRIAN. Well that's not a problem. You all think you have
problems. What are you addicted to, Jimmy? *(Grabbing
JIMMY's notebook.)* Let's see. I am addicted to jokes...Hi!
My name is Jimmy. I'm strong. I have to be because I
carry my mother to bed every night. And then I bench
press my grandmother. *(He throws JIMMY's notebook to
the floor.)*

JENNIFER. Hey, at least he came to school today to write
it...

JIMMY. Shut up, Jennifer.

BRIAN *(grabbing her notebook).* What are you addicted to,
Jennifer? No, wait, don't tell me. You're addicted to
school, right? Just can't get enough of it? *(He reads sarcastically.)* I am addicted to chewing gum.

JENNIFER. I didn't say you could read it!

BRIAN. Oh, that's a huge problem. People die from that all
the time. What's the worst that can happen to you? A few

cavities, a mild case of lockjaw? With all the people starving in the world, her biggest worry is whether to chew Wacky Watermelon or Goofy Grape! *(PAULA crosses to JENNIFER.)* Oh...so what...Paula's best friends with Jennifer now?

PAULA. I was just seeing if she was okay.

BRIAN. But that's your problem...So many notes to write, so many phone calls to make. I don't know how you fit it all in. Maybe that's why you have so many friends...Like Allen Heckman...Funny, he never mentioned you. Next thing you know, you're going to be best friends with Melissa!

MELISSA. I don't think so.

BRIAN. Why not? Isn't she popular enough for you, Ms. Popularity? Everybody's sweetheart. And would you believe she comes from a broken home? When did it first start falling apart for you, Melissa? Wasn't the new swimming pool big enough for you, or did your parents stop paying your Visa bill? Or maybe the chauffeur would only drive you to the mall once a week. These aren't problems!

MELISSA. I never said I had a problem!

BRIAN. That's right. You don't have a problem. None of us have problems!

*(The school bell rings, signaling the end of the period. The students return to their essays, quickly finishing up.)*

BRIAN. Brian D. Fenway. I am addicted to winning. My father always says play hard and achieve because once you get labeled a loser, it follows you the rest of your life. *(Freeze.)*

MELISSA. Melissa Ann Bainbridge. I am addicted to shopping. At the mall you can always get people to pay attention to you. They have to. It's their job. *(Freeze.)*

JENNIFER. Jennifer Scott. I am addicted to chewing gum. I chew over 50 pieces of gum a day. It's a big help when I want to lose a few pounds. *(Freeze.)*

JIMMY. Jimmy Joseph. I am addicted to jokes. I'm a very funny guy. No one wants to hear your problems. It's easier just to make them laugh. *(Freeze.)*

PAULA. Paula Dearborn. I am addicted to...I am addicted to fun. My friends are the most important people in the world. *(Freeze.)*

BRIAN *(stands)*. 3 p.m. Brian Fenway goes to football practice. He gets into a fight with a teammate who is frequently late. He has to sit out the big game. The team wins...without him. *(Goes into original freeze/pose.)*

MELISSA *(stands)*. 3:15. Melissa Ann Bainbridge gets caught stealing a pair of earrings at Marshall Fields. She calls her parents from the police station and waits for them to pick her up. She has a court date two weeks from today. *(Into original freeze/pose.)*

JENNIFER *(stands)*. 3:30. Jennifer Scott passes out on the sidewalk on the way to swim practice. This has happened twice. Her coach asks her not to compete in the meet on Saturday. *(Into original freeze/pose.)*

PAULA *(stands)*. 3:45. Paula Dearborn waits for Justin after school. He does not show up. She calls him several times. He does not return her calls. She convinces herself that he still cares. *(Into original freeze/pose.)*

JIMMY *(stands)*. 4:00. Jimmy Joseph arrives home to an empty house. He finds an empty bottle of vodka and the car keys gone. *(He begins to gather his books, and then notices the audience.)* That's not a problem. *(Begins to *leave. Turns back.)* That's not a problem. *(Turns and notices the rest of the class, frozen.)* None of us have problems! *(Turns and freezes. Music.)*

## THE END

## PRODUCTION NOTES

THE PLAY: *NO PROBLEM* is a play consisting of several scenes, taking place in both realistic time and in the past. All classroom scenes, unless noted, take place in the present. All non-classroom scenes are flashbacks. All the characters take turns assuming the roles of mother, brother, friend, etc., throughout these memory scenes. These character transitions should be as smooth as possible, as the play moves rapidly and the flow is extremely important.

In order for the play to be effective, heightened theatricality must be used. This, however, does not imply that the characters should ever be unbelievable or unsympathetic. Rather, the director should draw on theatrical conventions in the staging of the play. Some suggestions, taken from the original production, are given. Also, when necessary to clarify certain scenes, some of the blocking from the original production is used. This is meant, in no way, to limit possibilities or to imply that this is how the play must or should be done. The actors and director are limited only by the limits of their own imagination and creativity.

THE SET: Should be simple, consisting of five desks and chairs. There are two bookcases, one on each side of the stage, placed downstage. Each is set with props that will be used in the memory scenes.

# PROPERTY LIST

## JENNIFER

notebook, 2 pens
several school books
eye glasses
several packs of sugar-free gum

## JIMMY

notebook, pen
school bag
jacket

## PAULA

notebook, pen
letter stationery and envelopes

## BRIAN

notebook, pen
football jersey

## MELISSA

notebook, pen
fashion magazine
purse with make-up and hairbrush

## PROPERTIES FOR MEMORY SCENES

All properties for memory scenes are kept on bookshelves
until needed.

TV remote control
bag of potato chips
cordless telephone
baseball cap
shirt box (inside: small sweater and letter from Dad)
purse
bottle of whisky and glass
pair of earrings
Hair and Make-up Barbie doll
duffel bag filled with clothes and a towel

# *NO PROBLEM*

## SCENE DESIGN

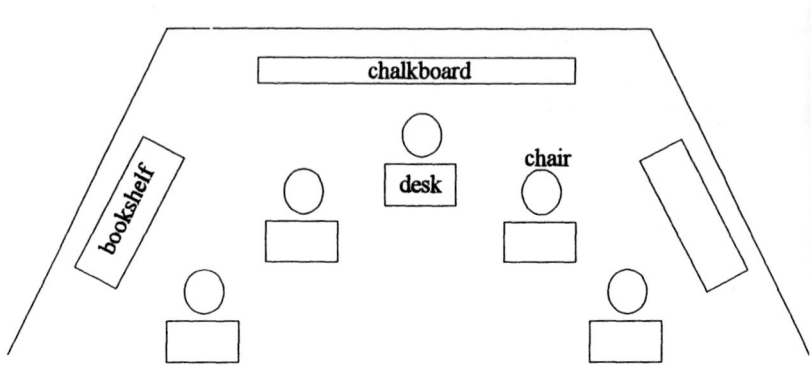

## CLASSROOM EXERCISES

The following exercises are designed to enourage independent thought, as well as discussion, about the issues raised in *NO PROBLEM*.

### DISCUSSION

1.  Why is the play entitled *NO PROBLEM*?

2.  How do the characters cover up their problems?
    Why don't they talk to their friends about their problems?
    Where could these characters go for help?

3.  Who, besides the characters themselves, are affected by the problems you saw in the play?

4.  Movies, television and magazines create "ideal" images of how we should look, act and feel. What role models and advertisements do you think might influence each particular character?

### WRITING

1.  Choose one character and write an honest essay for him/her on the topic "I am addicted to..."

2.  Write a letter to the character in the play you feel you have the most to say to.

3.  Select a character and write an entry in his/her journal, as that character might write.

4.  If these characters had the opportunity to write an honest letter to their parents, what might they say? Write that letter for one of the characters.

5.  Choose a character and describe, from their point of view, their favorite object and why it is important.

## CREATIVE DRAMATICS

1.  Problems happen when we don't express what we really want to say. Divide students into pairs, with one being a character from the play and the other being that person's parent. Create short scenes of conflict. Freeze the action after the verbal conflict. Allow each character to say what he/she "really wants to say."

Examples of scenes are:
a.  The first time Paula has dinner with her father after his remarriage
b.  A classmate of Jimmy's goes to his house after school to work on a homework assignment
c.  Melissa has a solo in the Spring Concert and her parents say they cannot attend because they must go to a benefit dinner
d.  Jennifer and her parents receive and open two letters on the same day. One is an acceptance from the Summer Honor's Program and the other is an offer for a lifeguarding job
e.  Brian has punched a hole in the wall after losing a football game and must explain it to his father

2.  Often the seeds of problems are planted long ago. Divide the students into groups of three or four. Invite them to plan

a still photograph of one of the characters when they were younger. The other members of the group can play parents, friends, or family members. Following the presentation of each of these three-dimensional pictures, talk about what feelings are represented, not just in what is happening but in what may happen in the future. One example might be watching Brian receive his first trophy with his parents watching.

3. Now let's move into the future. Divide the class into groups of five with each student representing a character from the play. Have the students improvise a class reunion ten years into the future. Give them time to plan what they will tell each other about what they are doing now. This could also be a writing project defined by 1) Where they are? 2) What they are doing? and 3) Who they are with? Remind your students that these do not have to be "happily ever after" scenes. Encourage your students to be sincere and honest.

## EXTENDED PROJECT

Plan a music video that captures one of the characters in the play, or one of the conflicts. What song would you use, and what images, to tell the story?

## FOR FURTHER READING

*Treating and Overcoming Anorexia Nervosa* by Steven Levenkron
*Femininity* by Susan Brownmiller
*The Obsession: Reflections of the Tryranny of Slenderness* by Kim Chernin
*The Best Little Girl in the World* by Steven Levenkron
*Alcoholism: A Family Illness* by Betty Ready
*Drinking Problem* by John E. Keller
*New Primer on Alcoholism* by Marty Mann

*The Drama of the Gifted Child* by Alice Miller

*On the Family: A Revolutionary Way of Self-Discovery* by John Bradshaw

*Hormonal Manipulation: A New Age of Monstrous Athletes* by William N. Taylor

*Shoplifting* by L.B. Taylor

*Facing Codependence* by Pia Mellody w/ Andrea Wells Miller and J. Keith Miller

*Breaking Free: A Recovery Workbook for Facing Codependence* by Pia Mellody

*Co-dependent No More: How to Stop Controlling Others and Start Caring for Yourself* by Mellody Beattie

*Breaking Free of the Co-dependency Trap* by Barry K. and Janae B. Weinnold

# DIRECTOR'S NOTES

# DIRECTOR'S NOTES

# DIRECTOR'S NOTES

# DIRECTOR'S NOTES

# DIRECTOR'S NOTES

# DIRECTOR'S NOTES